WORKBOOKS

1st Grade

Geography

Author Mark Shulman
Educational Consultant Kara Pranikoff

Editors Jolyon Goddard,
Cecile Landau, Rohini Deb,
Nancy Ellwood
Art Editor Tanvi Nathyal
Assistant Art Editor Kanika Kalra
Managing Editor Soma B. Chowdhury
Managing Art Editors Richard Czapnik,
Ahlawat Gunjan
Producer, Pre-Production Ben Marcus
Producer Christine Ni
DTP Designer Anita Yadav

First American Edition, 2015
Published in the United States by DK Publishing
345 Hudson Street, New York, New York 10014

A catalog record for this book
is available from the Library of Congress.
ISBN: 978-1-4654-2847-9

DK books are available at special discounts when purchased
in bulk for sales promotions, premiums, fund-raising, or
educational use. For details, contact: DK Publishing Special
Markets, 345 Hudson Street, New York, New York 10014
SpecialSales@dk.com

Printed and bound in Hong Kong

All images © Dorling Kindersley Limited
For further information see: www.dkimages.com

A WORLD OF IDEAS:
SEE ALL THERE IS TO KNOW

www.dk.com

Contents

This chart lists all the topics in the book.
Once you have completed each page,
stick a star in the correct box below.

Geography involves learning about the world around you. Geographers study both the natural world, and the way that humans use and change that world. When you look at a bridge across a river, you see both the natural and the human world. The river is part of the natural world. It was there long before people came to live near it. The bridge is part of the human world. People built the bridge to help them cross the river.

Use the words "natural" or "human" to complete the sentences below.

A mountain is part of the _Natural_ world.

A car tunnel is part of the _human_ world.

Write **N** next to the things that are part of the natural world.
Write **H** next to the things that form part of the human world.

 H

 N

N

 H

Very few places on Earth today have not been affected by human activity. Almost everywhere you look you will see things from both the natural world and the human world.

Look at the picture below. Label the objects that are part of the natural world with the word "Natural," and those that are part of the human world with the word "Human."

FACTS

We live on planet Earth. All planets, including Earth, are the shape of a sphere. A sphere is round in every direction, like a ball.

Circle the items that are spheres.

Tube

Coin

Orange

Baseball

Box

Dice

Pig

Marble

Maps are pictures that help us understand the world. They help us picture many kinds of places. Some maps show only the natural world. Other maps show the human world.

Use the words in the box to label the place shown on each of the maps below.

Bedroom   Country   City   Earth   Island   Mountain

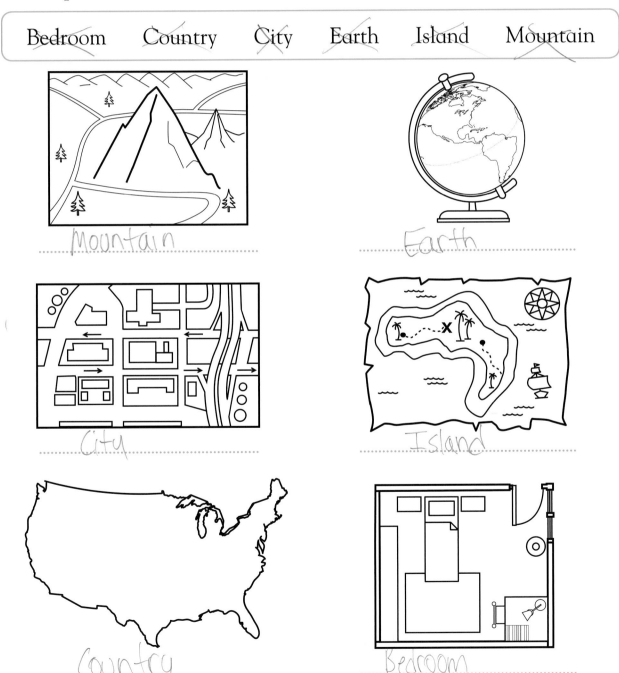

Mountain

Earth

City

Island

Country

Bedroom

FACTS

"North," "south," "east," and "west" are words that describe directions. These directions are often marked on a map with a shape called a compass rose. The compass rose tells you in which direction the top of the map is pointing. Most maps have north at the top and south at the bottom, with west on the left and east on the right. The compass rose does not always say north, south, east, and west. Often, it just says **N**, **S**, **E**, and **W**.

Look at the map below. Use the compass rose to answer the questions using the letters **N**, **S**, **E**, or **W**. Your starting point is the house in the middle of the map.

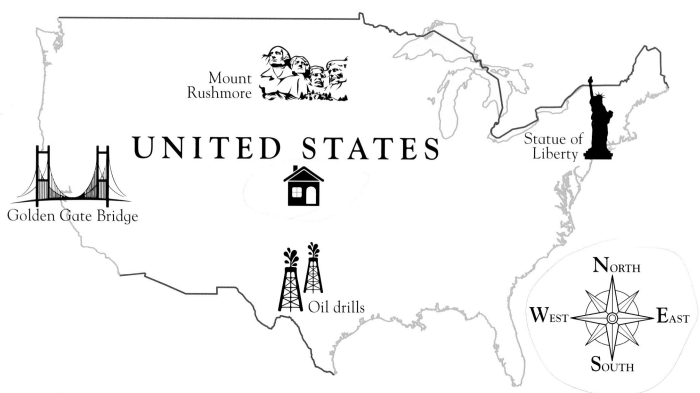

What direction will you travel from the house to the following places?

Oil drills in Texas   S   Statue of Liberty   E

Mount Rushmore   N   Golden Gate Bridge   W

There are seven very large areas of land on Earth. These are called continents. When you look at a map of Earth, you see the seven continents. They are Africa, Antarctica, Asia, Australia, Europe, North America, and South America.

Look at the map carefully and follow the instructions below.

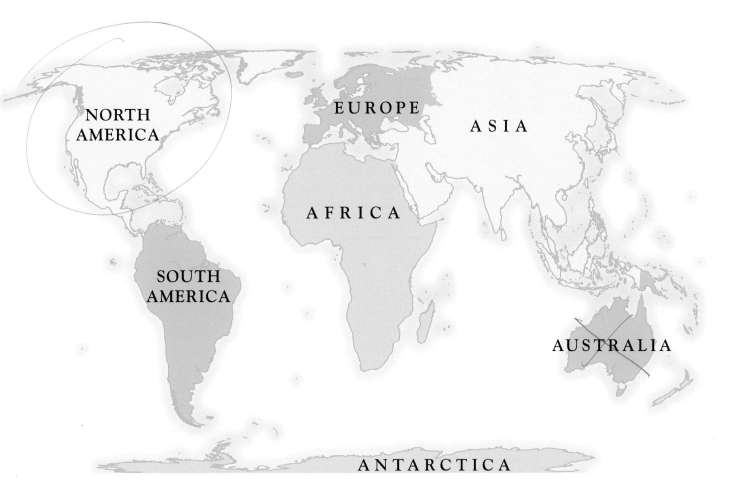

Name the largest continent. _Asia_

Put an X on the continent that is the smallest.

Find the continent you live on and circle it.

FACTS

The continent of North America has 23 countries. Of those countries, 12 are islands in the Caribbean Sea. There are seven small countries south of Mexico, which form the region called Central America. The three largest countries in North America are Canada, the United States of America, and Mexico.

Look at the map carefully and follow the instructions given below it.

Color Canada red.

Color the United States blue.

Color Mexico green.

The continent of South America is connected to North America. South America is divided into 12 countries. The largest country in South America is Brazil. The world's second longest river, the Amazon River, begins in the mountains of Peru and flows through northern Brazil.

Look at the map carefully and follow the instructions given below it.

Color Brazil green.

Color Peru red.

Find the Amazon River and circle it.

FACTS

The continent of Africa is divided into 54 countries. Africa has many wild areas. It has the world's hottest desert, the Sahara, and one of the world's biggest waterfalls, Victoria Falls. There is a huge rain forest around the Congo River. Africa's eastern grasslands are home to giraffes, lions, gazelles, and the African elephant, which is the world's largest animal that lives on land.

Use the map and its compass rose to help you complete the sentences below. Write "north," "south," "east," "west," or "center" in each blank space.

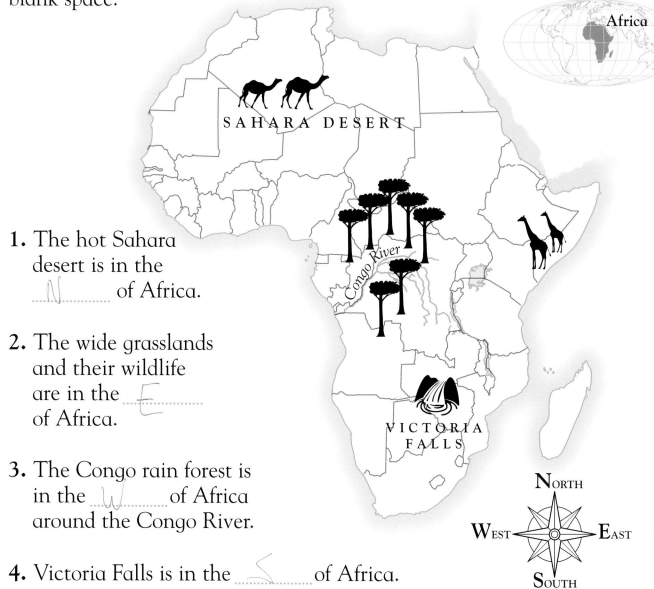

1. The hot Sahara desert is in the ___N___ of Africa.

2. The wide grasslands and their wildlife are in the ___E___ of Africa.

3. The Congo rain forest is in the ___W___ of Africa around the Congo River.

4. Victoria Falls is in the ___S___ of Africa.

Asia is the largest continent in the world. It has 49 countries and includes the world's largest country, Russia, which stretches all the way across the top of Asia. Asia is also home to the world's two most populated countries. They are China and India.

Look at the map of Asia and follow the instructions below it.

Write an **R** in Russia and draw a box around its name.
Write an **I** in India and draw a circle around its name.
Write a **C** in China and draw a triangle around its name.

The continents of Europe and Asia are connected. Europe is divided into 46 countries. Many languages are spoken in different countries of Europe.

Below is a list of five languages. Draw a line to connect each language to the country on the map where that language is spoken.

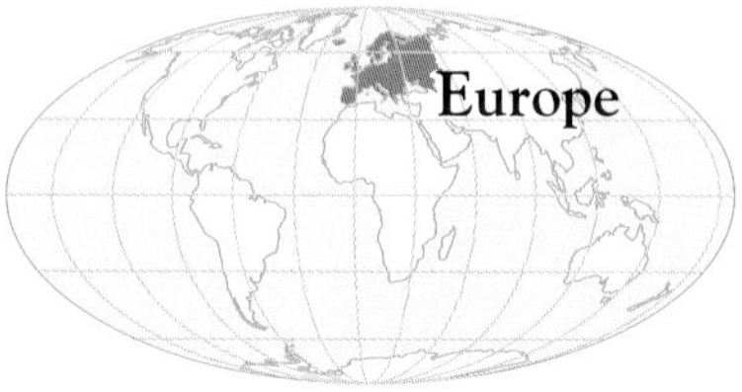

Europe

Languages

German

Greek

Italian

French

Spanish

GERMANY

FRANCE

SPAIN

ITALY

GREECE

FACTS

Australia is the smallest continent. It is also one single country. Many of Australia's native animals, such as kangaroos and koalas, do not live in the wild anywhere else on Earth. Australia is near 13 other island countries in the Pacific Ocean. Together, all of those countries are called Oceania.

Read the list of the names of four native Australian animals. Draw a line that connects each name to the picture of the animal on the map of Australia.

Australia

O C E A N I A

A U S T R A L I A

Animals

Kangaroo

Wombat

Koala

Squirrel glider

★ Antarctica

Antarctica is the continent covering the South Pole, the southernmost part of Earth. It is the coldest and the windiest continent. It is a land that is always covered in ice and snow. There are no countries in Antarctica. Nobody lives in Antarctica all the time. Most of the people who visit Antarctica are scientists and explorers.

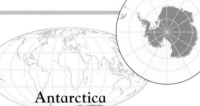

Antarctica

Look at the map of Antarctica below. Then, circle the items that you would need if you were visiting this cold continent.

ANTARCTICA

The equator is the imaginary line that runs around the middle of Earth, exactly halfway between the North Pole and the South Pole. The equator is at the widest part of Earth. Places on the equator are some of the hottest places on Earth.

Draw a line along the equator on the globe.

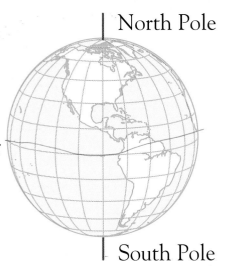

North Pole

Equator

South Pole

In the map below, color the three continents that the equator goes through.

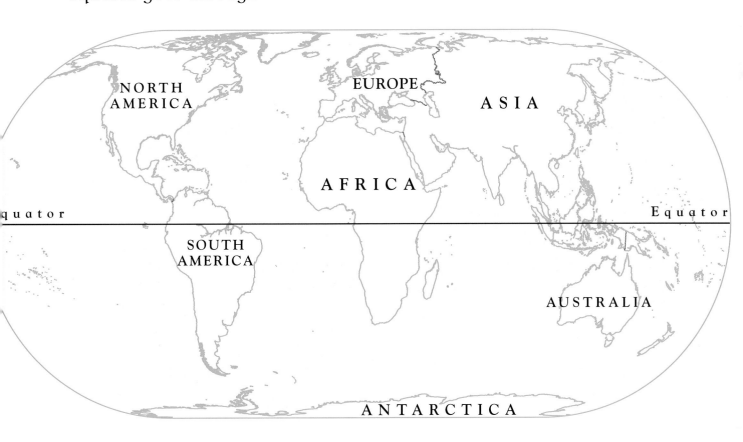

NORTH AMERICA

EUROPE

ASIA

AFRICA

Equator

SOUTH AMERICA

AUSTRALIA

ANTARCTICA

FACTS

Earth is a sphere, which means it is shaped like a ball. At the very top of Earth is the North Pole, and at the very bottom is the South Pole. The sun does not shine much at the poles. That is why they are very cold and icy. Would you like to live in a freezing place like that?

Below are some of the animals that live in the chilly regions around the poles. Three of them live in the Arctic region, around the North Pole, and one lives in Antarctica near the South Pole. Draw a circle around the animal that lives near the South Pole.

North Pole

South Pole

Polar bear

Penguin

Moose

Arctic fox

FACTS

Most of Earth is covered by water, and most of Earth's water is found in oceans. Oceans are the largest bodies of water in the world. There are five oceans on Earth—the Pacific Ocean, the Atlantic Ocean, the Indian Ocean, the Arctic Ocean, and the Southern Ocean.

Circle the animals that live in the ocean.

Whale

Walrus

Ostrich

Cow

Crab

Shark

Bear

Mouse

Sea turtle

FACTS

The Pacific Ocean is the world's largest body of water. It lies between four different continents. The Pacific Ocean is so large that it would take you many weeks to cross it in a sailboat. There are more volcanoes around the Pacific Ocean than anywhere else on Earth.

Look at the map below. Color the continents that touch the Pacific Ocean.

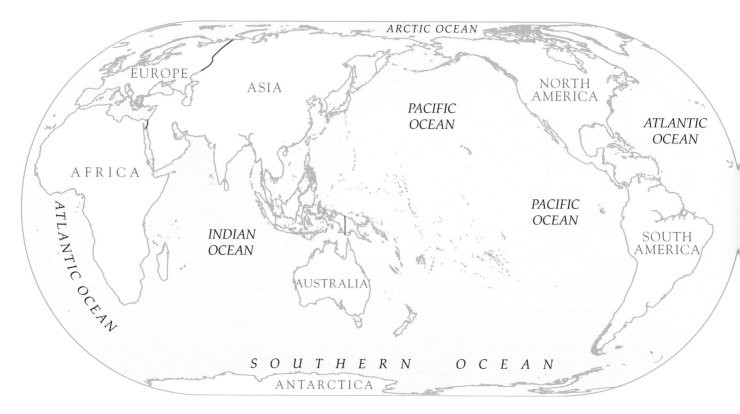

Read the sentences below. Circle the correct option in each sentence.

There are more volcanoes / trees around the Pacific Ocean than any other ocean on Earth.

The Pacific Ocean is the largest / smallest ocean in the world.

The Atlantic Ocean is the world's second-largest body of water. It lies between four different continents. The first European explorers and settlers to come to the United States sailed across the Atlantic Ocean.

Look at the map below. Color the continents that touch the Atlantic Ocean.

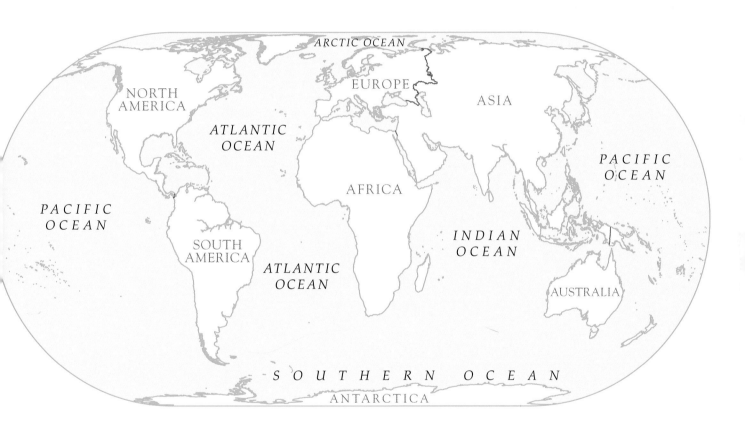

Read the sentences below. Circle the correct option in each sentence.

The Altantic Ocean is the largest / second-largest ocean in the world.

The first European explorers and settlers to come to the United States sailed across the Atlantic Ocean / Arctic Ocean.

FACTS

An island is an area of land that has water all around it. Islands are much smaller than continents. Islands do not float on the water. In fact, islands are like mountains that are mostly underwater. The US state of Hawaii is made up of islands.

Read the words in the box below. Use them to fill in the blanks in the sentences.

| float | hot | boat | fish |

Kauai

Niihau

Oahu

Molokai

Maui

Lanai

Kahoolawe

Hawaii

1. If you want to reach an island, you will need a ....

2. Islands are connected to Earth. They do not........................ .

3. If you live on an island, you might eat a lot of........................ .

4. Some islands are in places where the weather is ....

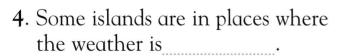

A lake is a large body of water completely surrounded by land. Lakes come in many sizes. Some lakes are very big. People often build houses, towns, and cities next to lakes. There are many different ways that people use lakes for pleasure, and to make their lives easier.

Look at the picture. Circle all the ways that people are using the lake.

Water always flows from high places to low places. A large amount of running water is called a river. A small amount of running water is called a stream. Some rivers are very long and very wide. Their water can move very quickly, too. Streams are usually much smaller than rivers.

Write an **R** in the box next to the picture of the river, and write an **S** in the box next to the picture of the stream.

Mountains and hills are areas of land that rise up higher than the land around them. Hills are not as high as mountains. Some mountains are so tall that they touch the cold air high above Earth. That is why some mountains have snow on them, even in warm weather.

Connect the dots in both of the pictures. Then, draw a snowman in the mountain scene and a house in the hill scene.

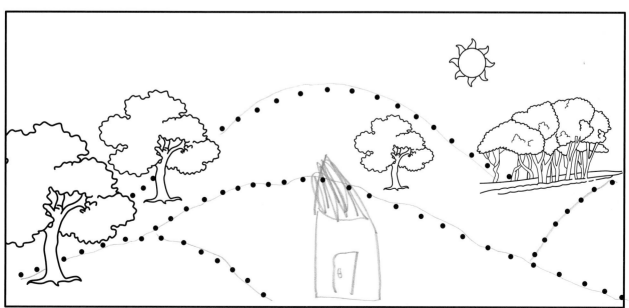

A forest is a large area of land covered with many trees. Many different kinds of plants grow under the tree cover. Wild animals, all of different sizes, live in forests. Bears, wolves, deer, chipmunks, raccoons, frogs, owls, and many other kinds of animals make their homes in forests. There are many forests on Earth.

Look at the pictures below, and put an **F** next to the things that you might expect to see in a forest.

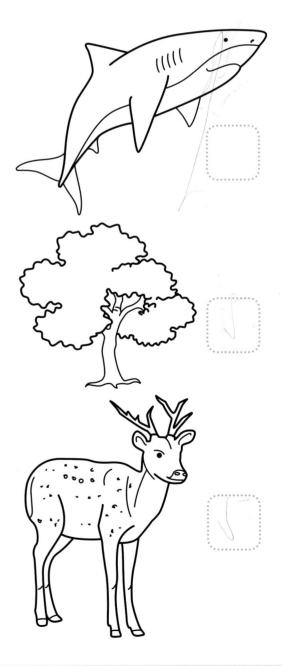

Jungles are very rainy and wet parts of Earth. Because of all the rain, jungles can support the growth of lots of different kinds of plants. Most of Earth's plants and animals are found in jungles. They are often very hot places. Jungles are usually hard places for people to live in.

Look at the pictures below and put a **J** next to the things that you might expect to see in a jungle.

A desert is a very dry part of the world that gets very little rain. Deserts can be very hot in the daytime and very cold at night. Some plants and animals manage to live in the desert, but it is not an easy place for people to live in.

Look at the pictures below, and put a **D** next to the things that you might expect to see in a hot desert.

Some maps show just the natural parts of Earth. Other maps show the places that humans have created. These kinds of maps are called political maps. They show countries, cities, and other types of places that are not part of the natural world.

Put a **P** in the box next to the kinds of places that would be on a political map. Put an **N** next to the kinds of places that would be on a map of the natural world.

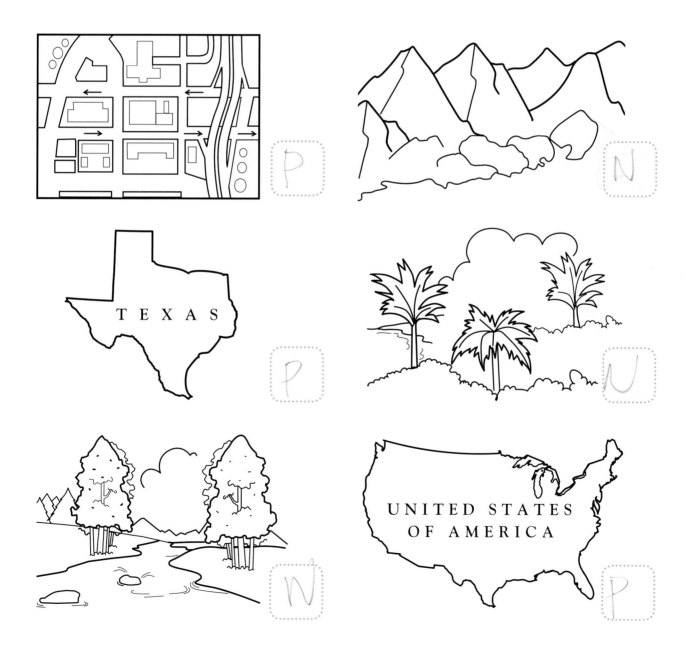

TEXAS

UNITED STATES OF AMERICA

Earth is divided into about 200 countries. Some countries are very big and some are very small. The five largest countries by size are Russia, Canada, the United States, China, and Brazil. The two largest countries by population are China and India.

Look at this map of the world. Then, follow the instructions below. You can ask an adult for help.

Find the country you live in on the map. What is the name of your country?

....

Name the country that is both one of the five largest countries by size and one of the two largest by population.

....

Write the names of the three largest countries in order of their size.

1. ....

2. ....

3. ....

In a country, all the people share the same leaders and government. Generally, most of the people in a country speak the same language and have many things in common.

Sometimes, a country has a natural border that is created by an ocean or sea. Other times, a country's border can be a river or mountains. Sometimes the borders are created by people. Those man-made borders usually look like a straight line on a map.

Here is a map showing the 12 countries of South America. Draw a blue line on the border of every country. In red, color the two countries that do not have a border on an ocean or sea.

Some countries are divided into areas called provinces. Canada, the world's second-largest country, is divided into 10 provinces. The country also has three large areas called territories, close to the North Pole. The Yukon Territory, the Northwest Territories, and Nunavut are Canada's three territories.

Look at this map of Canada, and then follow the instructions below.

Color the only Canadian province that borders the Pacific Ocean.

Draw a warm, winter hat in the Northwest Territories.

Draw mittens in the Yukon Territory.

Draw snowflakes in Nunavut.

FACTS

Some large countries, such as the United States of America, are divided into smaller areas called states. Some states, such as California and Texas, are very large. Other states, such as Rhode Island and Delaware, are very small.

Here is a map of the United States.

Color in green the four states whose names start with the word "New."

The names of eight states begin with the letter "M." Color them blue.

The names of four states begin with an "A." Color them red.

If you live in the US, put a check (✓) on your state. If you do not, check (✓) the state you would most like to visit.

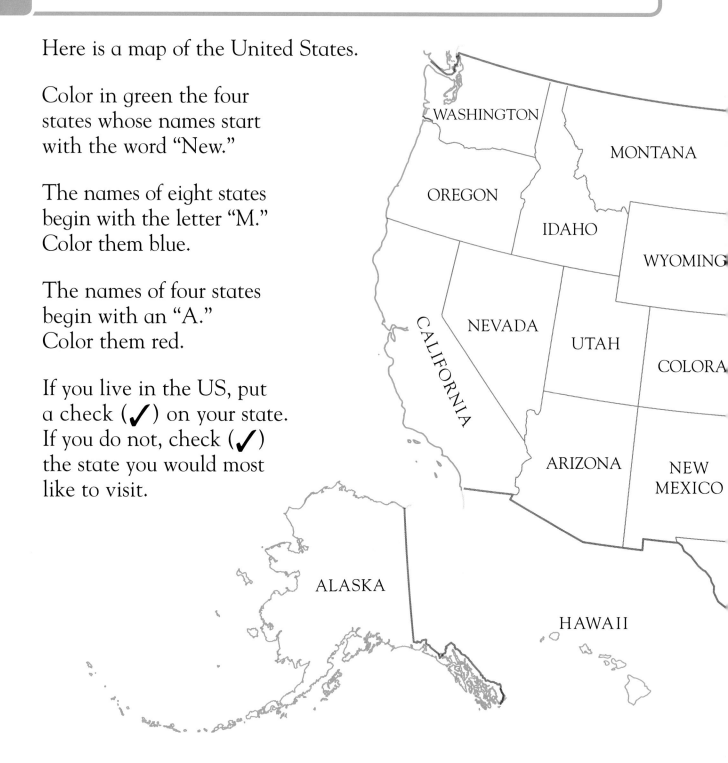

The United States of America is often called the United States or just the US. It is divided into 50 states. Forty-eight of them share borders with at least one other state on the North American continent. They make up the continental United States. Two states, Alaska and Hawaii, are not connected to the other 48 states.

A city is a place where many people live near each other. In a city, there are many big buildings, houses, schools, parks, and roads. A city has museums, sports teams, theaters, and many things for people to do. Cities are large places, so there are many ways to travel in a city. People living in cities mostly work in offices and factories, not on farms or agricultural land.

Circle the different ways people travel in a city.
Cross out the ways people do not usually travel in a city.
Put a check (✓) next to the ways you would like to travel when you are in a city.

Cities come in different sizes. Some cities are very large, with millions of people. Other cities are not as large. A map can show you which cities are large and which cities are small. On a map, the names of the largest cities have the biggest letters.

Here is a map of three states in the US—California, Oregon, and Washington. Circle the names of the large cities in these states.

Every country has a capital city. Leaders and the government meet in the capital city to do their work. States and provinces have capital cities, too. Capitals are not always the largest cities in a state or country. They are shown on a map by a dot that is different from the dots showing other cities.

Here is a map of the US showing three states—California, Oregon, and Washington. Circle the capital city of each state. **Hint:** In this map, the capitals are marked by stars.

FACTS

A town is an area where people live near each other. It is smaller than a city and usually has smaller buildings. A town also has fewer people than a city. Many people choose to live in towns because they do not want to live in a big city.

Check (✔) the pictures of places you would find in a town.
Put an ✗ next to the pictures of places you would find in a city.

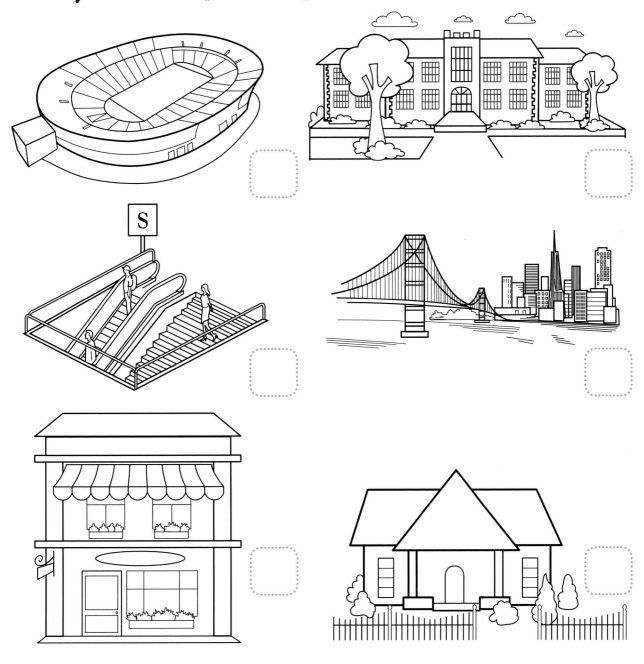

Map Keys and Symbols

Maps use symbols to show different kinds of buildings and other features. These symbols are usually pictures that represent the things that they show. All the symbols used on a map, and what they represent, are shown in a map key.

Match each map symbol to the word it is showing.

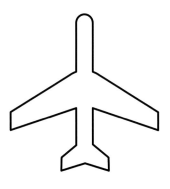

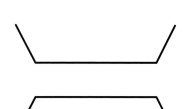

Hospital

Mountain

Bridge

Farm

Airport

Restaurant

Road

River

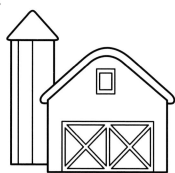

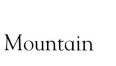

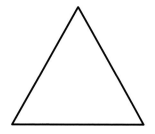

A Park Map ⭐

A map can help you find your way around a place, such as a park. The park map on this page uses symbols to tell people what activities they can do in the park.

Using the words from the box, label each symbol on the map with what that symbol represents. Then, use the compass rose to help you answer the questions below the map.

Snack bar	Gift shop	Parking lot	Bathroom
	Park office	Swimming pool	Playground

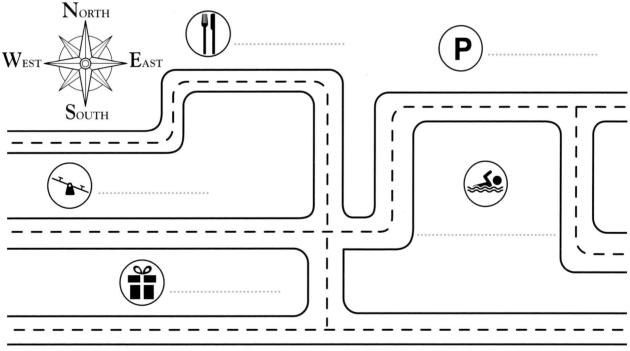

If you are at the playground and you want to go to the swimming pool, what direction will you go?

If you are at the snack bar and you want to go to the bathroom, what direction will you go?

★ A Nature Map

A nature map tells you about an area of land. Each of the symbols in the key shows a different part of the natural world. The map helps you plan where you want to go.

Using the words from the box, label the different kinds of places from the natural world that are shown on the map. Then, use the compass rose to help you answer the questions below the map.

Beach	Waterfall	Forest	Mountains
Hills	Lake	River	

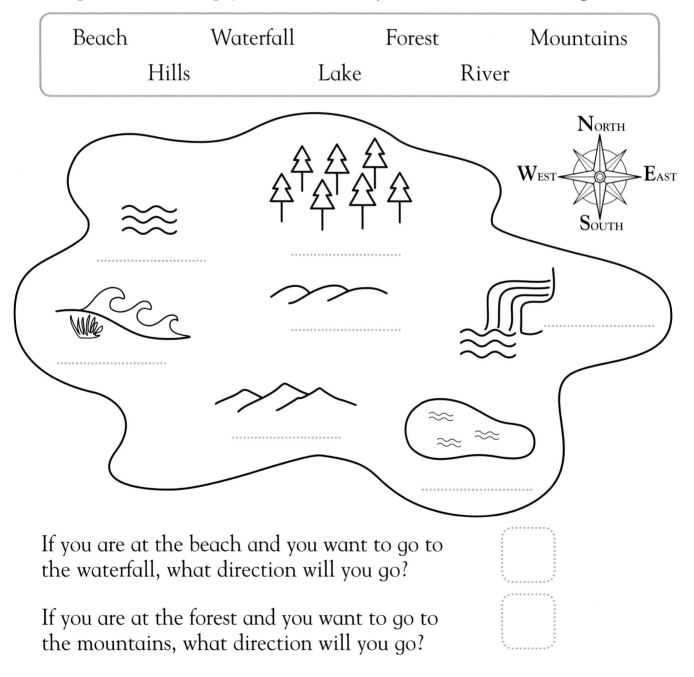

If you are at the beach and you want to go to the waterfall, what direction will you go?

If you are at the forest and you want to go to the mountains, what direction will you go?

A neighborhood map often uses pictures of buildings as its symbols. This kind of map is helpful for finding the places you want to visit in a town.

Imagine you are traveling from your home to your school. You are going to make a few stops on the way. You are going to stop at these places in the order given in the word box below.

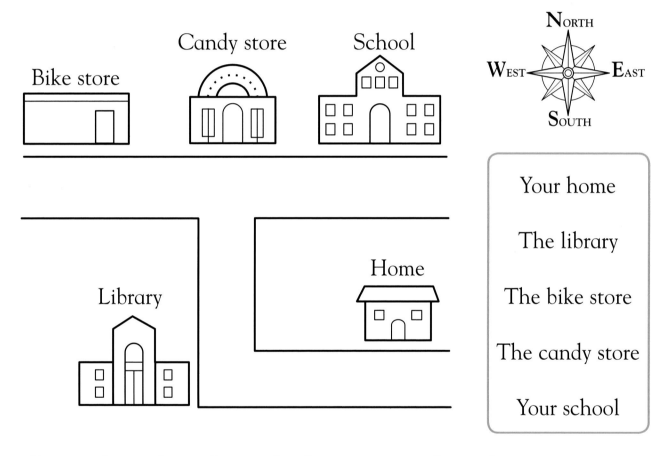

Your home

The library

The bike store

The candy store

Your school

Draw a line, along the roads, that connects these places in the order you will visit them.

To go from the bike store to your school, what direction will you go?

To go from the library to the candy store, what direction will you go?

Not all maps use picture symbols. In this map of a school, each of the different areas uses letters to tell you what you can find there.

Point at each location on the map and say its name aloud, using the key to find its name. Circle the names of your two favorite places. Then, use the compass rose to help you answer the questions below the map.

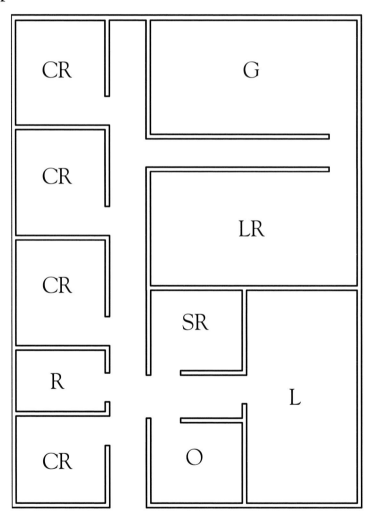

Key	
LR	Lunch room
O	Office
SR	Science room
L	Library
G	Gym
R	Restroom
CR	Classroom

If you are at the library and want to go to the restroom, in what direction will you go?

If you are at the gym and want to go to the lunch room, in what direction will you go?

A map is a plan that can help you describe a place. Everyone can make a map. Look at the world around you. You can use simple symbols or letters to describe a place to other people. You can show the things they will find there.

Make a map of your bedroom by using any of the symbols in the key below. Draw them in the box and label them. You can add your own symbols for anything in your room that is not in the key.

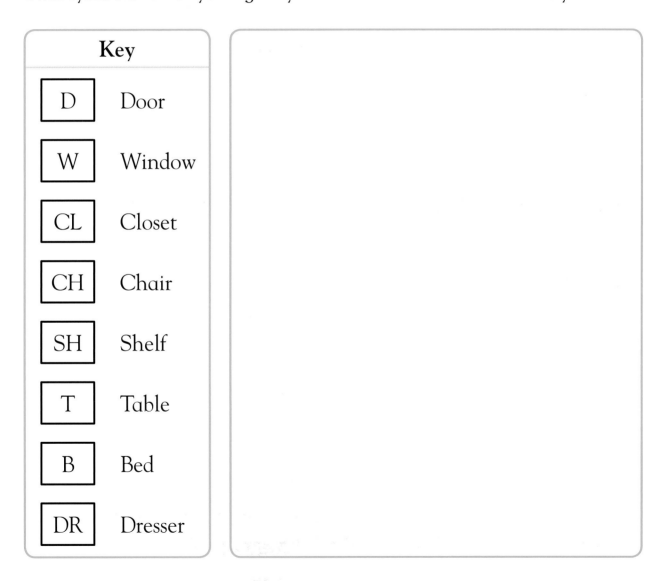

Key	
D	Door
W	Window
CL	Closet
CH	Chair
SH	Shelf
T	Table
B	Bed
DR	Dresser

If your bedroom is a different shape from this one, use another piece of paper to draw walls that match the shape of your bedroom.

Map Your Classroom

FACTS

A classroom is a place to learn. The objects in a classroom help children learn together.

Make a map of your classroom in the box below, using the symbols in the key. Create your own symbols for anything in your classroom that is missing from the key.

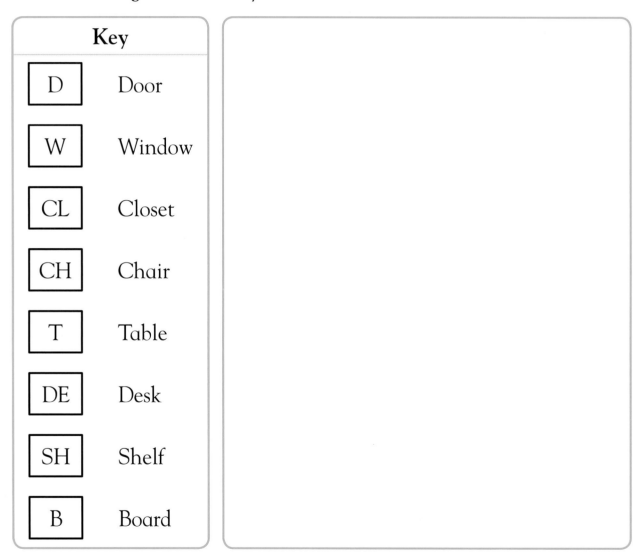

Key

D	Door
W	Window
CL	Closet
CH	Chair
T	Table
DE	Desk
SH	Shelf
B	Board

If your classroom is a different shape from this one, use another piece of paper to draw walls that match its shape.

Draw a symbol for yourself, to mark the place where you usually sit.

There are all kinds of neighborhoods. Some neighborhoods have many different kinds of buildings. Others may have very few buildings. A map of your neighborhood can help you understand the things you find there. It can help you describe your neighborhood to a friend.

Imagine the square in the middle of the box below is the home you live in. Draw your neighborhood around where you live. Include squares for buildings like a school or a supermarket.

Your home

What kind of building is your home? Color the middle square the same color as your real home.

On your map, which two buildings are closest to your home? Color those two squares the same color as the real buildings.

Certificate

Congratulations to

....

for successfully finishing this book.

1st Grade

GOOD JOB!

You're a star.

Date

....

Answer Section with Parents' Notes

This book is intended to support the geography concepts that are taught to your child in first grade. It includes activities that test your child's knowledge of the world around him or her. By working through this book, your child will be able to learn basic geography concepts in a fun and informative way.

Contents

These activities are intended to be completed by a child with adult support. The topics covered are as follows:
- The natural and the human (man-made) world;
- Bodies of water such as oceans, rivers, and lakes;
- Landforms such as mountains, hills, islands, deserts;
- Forests and jungles;
- Types of maps and their keys;
- Compass directions;
- Continents, countries, provinces, and territories;
- Cities and towns;
- The United States of America.

How to Help Your Child

As you work through the pages with your child, make sure he or she understands what each activity requires. Read the facts and instructions aloud. Encourage questions and reinforce observations that will build confidence and increase active participation in classes at school.

By working with your child, you will understand how he or she thinks and learns. When appropriate, use props and objects from daily life to help your child make connections with the world outside.

If an activity seems too challenging for your child, encourage him or her to try another page. You can also give encouragement by praising progress made as a correct answer is given and a page is completed.
Good luck and remember to have fun!

★ Geography

FACTS

Geography involves learning about the world around you. Geographers study both the natural world, and the way that humans use and change that world. When you look at a bridge across a river, you see both the natural and the human world. The river is part of the natural world. It was there long before people came to live near it. The bridge is part of the human world. People built the bridge to help them cross the river.

Use the words "natural" or "human" to complete the sentences below.

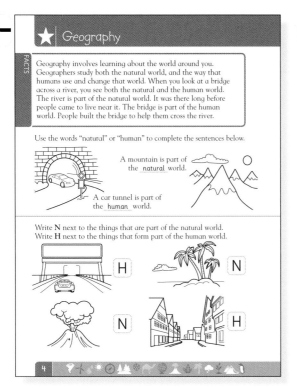

A mountain is part of the _natural_ world.

A car tunnel is part of the _human_ world.

Write **N** next to the things that are part of the natural world.
Write **H** next to the things that form part of the human world.

H N N H

As an extension to this activity, look at pictures in books, magazines, or on the internet with your child. Point to objects and ask him or her whether each one is part of the natural world or has been made by humans.

Your World ★

FACTS

Very few places on Earth today have not been affected by human activity. Almost everywhere you look you will see things from both the natural world and the human world.

Look at the picture below. Label the objects that are part of the natural world with the word "Natural," and those that are part of the human world with the word "Human."

Natural
Human
Natural
Human
Natural
Human
Human
Natural

You can continue this activity next time you go outside with your child. Point at buildings, cars, trees, or birds and ask whether they are part of the natural or the human world.

★ Earth

FACTS

We live on planet Earth. All planets, including Earth, are the shape of a sphere. A sphere is round in every direction, like a ball.

Circle the items that are spheres.

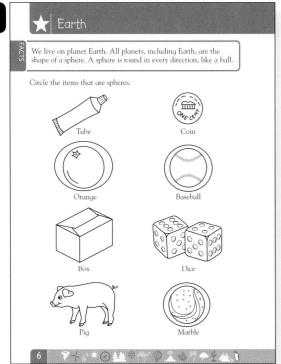

Tube   Coin

Orange   Baseball

Box   Dice

Pig   Marble

Combine this exercise with that on the previous page by asking your child whether the spherical objects mentioned on this page—Earth, orange, baseball, and marble—are natural or man-made.

Maps ★

FACTS

Maps are pictures that help us understand the world. They help us picture many kinds of places. Some maps show only the natural world. Other maps show the human world.

Use the words in the box to label the place shown on each of the maps below.

| Bedroom | Country | City | Earth | Island | Mountain |

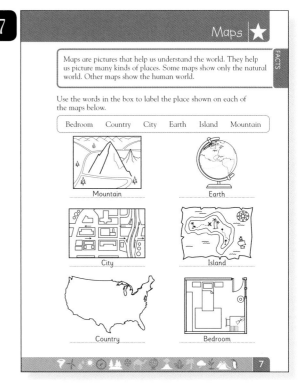

Mountain   Earth

City   Island

Country   Bedroom

You could reinforce the idea of maps by sketching a "treasure map" of your home, drawing crosses on places where you have hidden objects for your child to find.

★ Compass Directions

FACTS

"North," "south," "east," and "west" are words that describe directions. These directions are often marked on a map with a shape called a compass rose. The compass rose tells you in which direction the top of the map is pointing. Most maps have north at the top and south at the bottom, with west on the left and east on the right. The compass rose does not always say north, south, east, and west. Often, it just says **N**, **S**, **E**, and **W**.

Look at the map below. Use the compass rose to answer the questions using the letters **N**, **S**, **E**, or **W**. Your starting point is the house in the middle of the map.

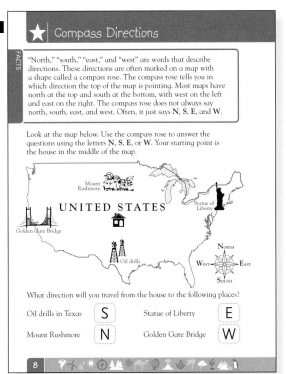

Mount Rushmore

UNITED STATES

Statue of Liberty

Golden Gate Bridge

Oil drills

NORTH
WEST   EAST
SOUTH

What direction will you travel from the house to the following places?

Oil drills in Texas   **S**   Statue of Liberty   **E**

Mount Rushmore   **N**   Golden Gate Bridge   **W**

Sketch a compass rose and ask your child to complete it by adding the directions, using **N** for "north," **S** for "south," and so on. Look outside a window together and tell your child which direction you are looking at, if you know. Having a compass with you will be handy!

Continents ★

FACTS

There are seven very large areas of land on Earth. These are called continents. When you look at a map of Earth, you see the seven continents. They are Africa, Antarctica, Asia, Australia, Europe, North America, and South America.

Look at the map carefully and follow the instructions below.

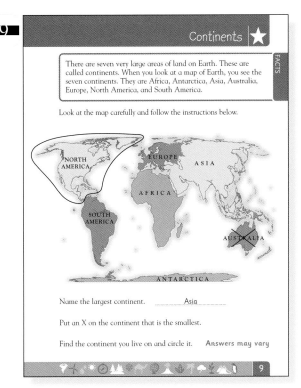

NORTH AMERICA   EUROPE   ASIA

AFRICA

SOUTH AMERICA

AUSTRALIA

ANTARCTICA

Name the largest continent. _____ Asia _____

Put an X on the continent that is the smallest.

Find the continent you live on and circle it.   **Answers may vary**

As an extra activity after completing this page, ask your child if he or she can recall the names of any of the seven continents. If this is too difficult, offer clues such as, "Kangaroos and koalas come from this continent."

★ North America

FACTS

The continent of North America has 23 countries. Of those countries, 12 are islands in the Caribbean Sea. There are seven small countries south of Mexico, which form the region called Central America. The three largest countries in North America are Canada, the United States of America, and Mexico.

Look at the map carefully and follow the instructions given below it.

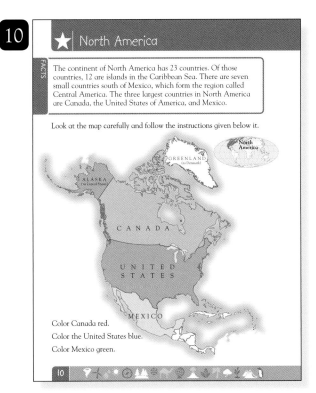

North America

GREENLAND
(to Denmark)

ALASKA
(to United States)

CANADA

UNITED STATES

MEXICO

Color Canada red.
Color the United States blue.
Color Mexico green.

After this exercise, talk about some of the other countries in North America, mentioning well-known natural or man-made landmarks you may know about, such as the Panama Canal, or the Rio Grande River.

South America ★

FACTS

The continent of South America is connected to North America. South America is divided into 12 countries. The largest country in South America is Brazil. The world's second longest river, the Amazon River, begins in the mountains of Peru and flows through northern Brazil.

Look at the map carefully and follow the instructions given below it.

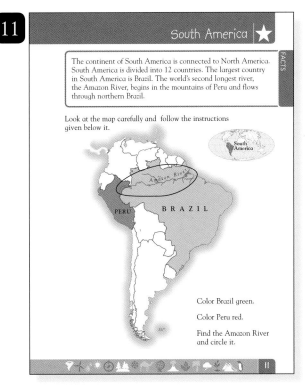

South America

Amazon River

PERU   BRAZIL

Color Brazil green.

Color Peru red.

Find the Amazon River and circle it.

You could also tell your child about the Amazon rain forest and how it is home to a great many animals and plants. You could also mention other countries in South America, such as Argentina and Chile, not labeled on the page.

★ Africa

The continent of Africa is divided into 54 countries. Africa has many wild areas. It has the world's hottest desert, the Sahara, and one of the world's biggest waterfalls, Victoria Falls. There is a huge rain forest around the Congo River. Africa's eastern grasslands are home to giraffes, lions, gazelles, and the African elephant, which is the world's largest animal that lives on land.

Use the map and its compass rose to help you complete the sentences below. Write "north," "south," "east," "west," or "center" in each blank space.

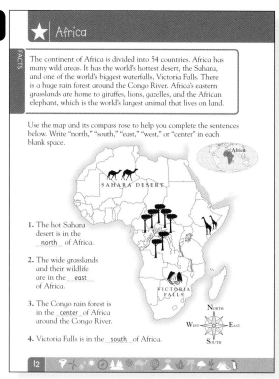

1. The hot Sahara desert is in the __north__ of Africa.

2. The wide grasslands and their wildlife are in the __east__ of Africa.

3. The Congo rain forest is in the __center__ of Africa around the Congo River.

4. Victoria Falls is in the __south__ of Africa.

It will be interesting to share with your child that some of the most famous animals come from Africa, including rhinoceroses, lions, giraffes, African elephants, and more. Do you have friends or family from Africa? Discuss with your child.

Asia ★

Asia is the largest continent in the world. It has 49 countries and includes the world's largest country, Russia, which stretches all the way across the top of Asia. Asia is also home to the world's two most populated countries. They are China and India.

Look at the map of Asia and follow the instructions below it.

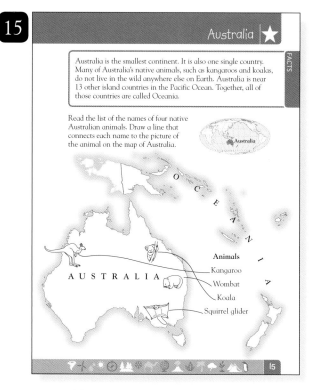

Write an **R** in Russia and draw a box around its name.
Write an **I** in India and draw a circle around its name.
Write a **C** in China and draw a triangle around its name.

Point out to your child that Russia is a country that spans both Europe and Asia. You could also point out other regions of Asia, such as the Middle East, Central Asia, and Southeast Asia. Do you have friends or family from Asia? Discuss with your child.

★ Europe

The continents of Europe and Asia are connected. Europe is divided into 46 countries. Many languages are spoken in different countries of Europe.

Below is a list of five languages. Draw a line to connect each language to the country on the map where that language is spoken.

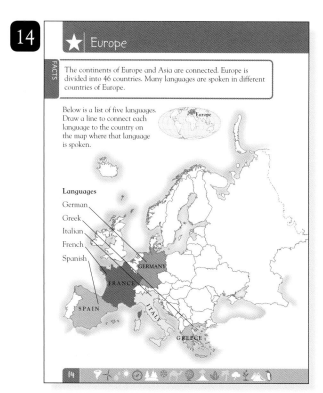

Languages
German
Greek
Italian
French
Spanish

Do you have family or friends from Europe? Discuss with your child that many people from Europe came to settle in the United States.

Australia ★

Australia is the smallest continent. It is also one single country. Many of Australia's native animals, such as kangaroos and koalas, do not live in the wild anywhere else on Earth. Australia is near 13 other island countries in the Pacific Ocean. Together, all of those countries are called Oceania.

Read the list of the names of four native Australian animals. Draw a line that connects each name to the picture of the animal on the map of Australia.

Animals
Kangaroo
Wombat
Koala
Squirrel glider

You could mention to your child that marsupials, such as wombats, kangaroos, and koalas, carry and protect their young in a pouch of skin, unlike the more familiar mammals, such as cats, dogs, and horses, he or she may know.

★ Antarctica

FACTS

Antarctica is the continent covering the South Pole, the southernmost part of Earth. It is the coldest and the windiest continent. It is a land that is always covered in ice and snow. There are no countries in Antarctica. Nobody lives in Antarctica all the time. Most of the people who visit Antarctica are scientists and explorers.

Look at the map of Antarctica below. Then, circle the items that you would need if you were visiting this cold continent.

Antarctica

ANTARCTICA

Your child may know very little about Antarctica. Explain that it was discovered by explorers less than 200 years ago, and that scientists from around the world travel there each year to do research.

Equator ★

FACTS

The equator is the imaginary line that runs around the middle of Earth, exactly halfway between the North Pole and the South Pole. The equator is at the widest part of Earth. Places on the equator are some of the hottest places on Earth.

Draw a line along the equator on the globe.

North Pole

Equator

South Pole

In the map below, color the three continents that the equator goes through.

NORTH AMERICA

EUROPE

ASIA

AFRICA

Equator

Equator

SOUTH AMERICA

AUSTRALIA

ANTARCTICA

You could tell your child that because the equator is hot all year round, there are no distinct seasons there. No spring, summer, fall, or winter. However, there are still cold places, such as high up in the snow-capped mountains of Ecuador.

★ North and South Poles

FACTS

Earth is a sphere, which means it is shaped like a ball. At the very top of Earth is the North Pole, and at the very bottom is the South Pole. The sun does not shine much at the poles. That is why they are very cold and icy. Would you like to live in a freezing place like that?

Below are some of the animals that live in the chilly regions around the poles. Three of them live in the Arctic region, around the North Pole, and one lives in Antarctica near the South Pole. Draw a circle around the animal that lives near the South Pole.

North Pole

South Pole

Polar bear

Penguin

Moose

Arctic fox

Share with your child that the North Pole is in the middle of the ice-covered Arctic Ocean, while the South Pole lies on land, on the continent of Antarctica. The nearest land to the North Pole is more than 400 miles away!

Oceans ★

FACTS

Most of Earth is covered by water, and most of Earth's water is found in oceans. Oceans are the largest bodies of water in the world. There are five oceans on Earth—the Pacific Ocean, the Atlantic Ocean, the Indian Ocean, the Arctic Ocean, and the Southern Ocean.

Circle the animals that live in the ocean.

Whale

Walrus

Ostrich

Cow

Crab

Shark

Bear

Mouse

Sea turtle

Ask your child if he or she knows the difference between freshwater and saltwater. If you have visited the beach, ask him or her to describe the animals and plants that live in and around the sea.

★ Pacific Ocean

The Pacific Ocean is the world's largest body of water. It lies between four different continents. The Pacific Ocean is so large that it would take you many weeks to cross it in a sailboat. There are more volcanoes around the Pacific Ocean than anywhere else on Earth.

Look at the map below. Color the continents that touch the Pacific Ocean.

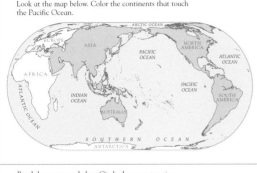

Read the sentences below. Circle the correct option in each sentence.

There are more (volcanoes) / trees around the Pacific Ocean than any other ocean on Earth.

The Pacific Ocean is the (largest) / smallest ocean in the world.

Your child may be interested to know that the Pacific Ocean contains the Mariana Trench. With a depth of almost 7 miles, the trench is the deepest part in all of the world's oceans.

Atlantic Ocean ★

The Atlantic Ocean is the world's second-largest body of water. It lies between four different continents. The first European explorers and settlers to come to the United States sailed across the Atlantic Ocean.

Look at the map below. Color the continents that touch the Atlantic Ocean.

Read the sentences below. Circle the correct option in each sentence.

The Atlantic Ocean is the largest / (second-largest) ocean in the world.

The first European explorers and settlers to come to the United States sailed across the (Atlantic Ocean) / Arctic Ocean.

After completing the activity on this page, cover the book and ask your child if he or she can remember the names of three of the four continents that touch the Atlantic Ocean. Help your child if he or she cannot remember.

★ Islands

An island is an area of land that has water all around it. Islands are much smaller than continents. Islands do not float on the water. In fact, islands are like mountains that are mostly underwater. The US state of Hawaii is made up of islands.

Read the words in the box below. Use them to fill in the blanks in the sentences.

float	hot	boat	fish

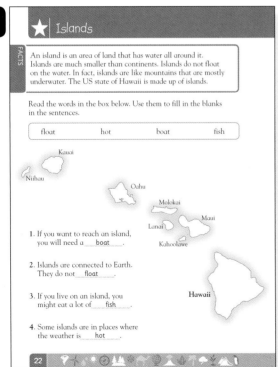

1. If you want to reach an island, you will need a ___boat___.

2. Islands are connected to Earth. They do not ___float___.

3. If you live on an island, you might eat a lot of ___fish___.

4. Some islands are in places where the weather is ___hot___.

Expand your child's knowledge by discussing any islands you may have visited, read about, or seen on television. You could also mention some well-known islands, such as the British Isles, Japan, Cuba, Puerto Rico, and Easter Island.

Lakes ★

A lake is a large body of water completely surrounded by land. Lakes come in many sizes. Some lakes are very big. People often build houses, towns, and cities next to lakes. There are many different ways that people use lakes for pleasure, and to make their lives easier.

Look at the picture. Circle all the ways that people are using the lake.

You could expand on the topic of lakes by telling your child about the five Great Lakes—Superior, Michigan, Huron, Erie, and Ontario—on the border between the United States and Canada. They are among the biggest lakes in the world.

★ Rivers

FACTS

Water always flows from high places to low places. A large amount of running water is called a river. A small amount of running water is called a stream. Some rivers are very long and very wide. Their water can move very quickly, too. Streams are usually much smaller than rivers.

Write an **R** in the box next to the picture of the river, and write an **S** in the box next to the picture of the stream.

Ask your child if he or she knows the names of some rivers. If not, mention the river nearest to where you live and how people use it. You could also mention some of the world's largest rivers, such as the Amazon, Mississippi, and Nile Rivers.

Mountains and Hills ★

FACTS

Mountains and hills are areas of land that rise up higher than the land around them. Hills are not as high as mountains. Some mountains are so tall that they touch the cold air high above Earth. That is why some mountains have snow on them, even in warm weather.

Connect the dots in both of the pictures. Then, draw a snowman in the mountain scene and a house in the hill scene.

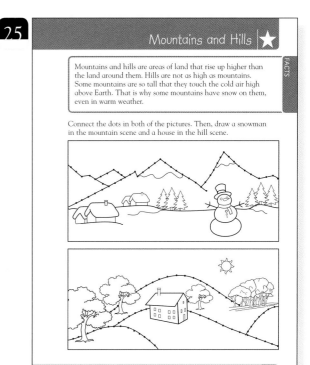

Next time you travel with your child, point to some hills and animals that might live there. If you are lucky enough to see mountains, point to them, too. Tell your child the name of the tallest mountain in your country or continent, if you know it.

★ Forests

FACTS

A forest is a large area of land covered with many trees. Many different kinds of plants grow under the tree cover. Wild animals, all of different sizes, live in forests. Bears, wolves, deer, chipmunks, raccoons, frogs, owls, and many other kinds of animals make their homes in forests. There are many forests on Earth.

Look at the pictures below, and put an **F** next to the things that you might expect to see in a forest.

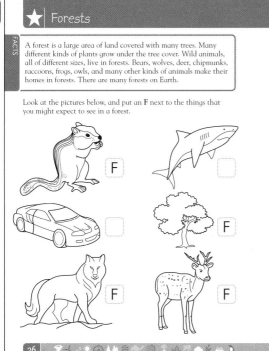

Explain to your child that people often built towns near forests because the trees provided the wood for buildings and furniture.

Jungles ★

FACTS

Jungles are very rainy and wet parts of Earth. Because of all the rain, jungles can support the growth of lots of different kinds of plants. Most of Earth's plants and animals are found in jungles. They are often very hot places. Jungles are usually hard places for people to live in.

Look at the pictures below and put a **J** next to the things that you might expect to see in a jungle.

Jungles include the tropical forests that are home to a huge number of different plants and animals. You could also explain to your child that many jungles are under threat as the trees are being cleared to make farmland or for timber.

★ Deserts

FACTS

A desert is a very dry part of the world that gets very little rain. Deserts can be very hot in the daytime and very cold at night. Some plants and animals manage to live in the desert, but it is not an easy place for people to live in.

Look at the pictures below, and put a **D** next to the things that you might expect to see in a hot desert.

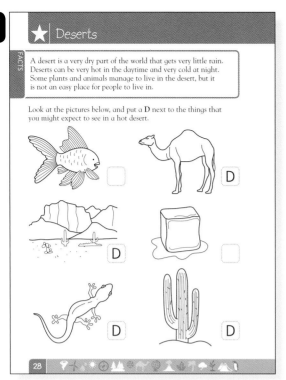

Use books or the internet to find out about one of the deserts in North America, such as the Mojave Desert. What kind of animals and plants live there? Are there any towns in the desert?

Political Maps ★

FACTS

Some maps show just the natural parts of Earth. Other maps show the places that humans have created. These kinds of maps are called political maps. They show countries, cities, and other types of places that are not part of the natural world.

Put a **P** in the box next to the kinds of places that would be on a political map. Put an **N** next to the kinds of places that would be on a map of the natural world.

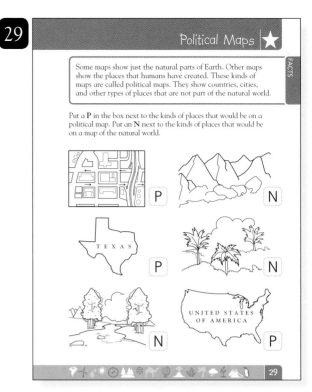

After working through this page, introduce your child to an atlas—if you have one at home. Show him or her the city or town you live in.

★ Countries

FACTS

Earth is divided into about 200 countries. Some countries are very big and some are very small. The five largest countries by size are Russia, Canada, the United States, China, and Brazil. The two largest countries by population are China and India.

Look at this map of the world. Then, follow the instructions below. You can ask an adult for help.

Find the country you live in on the map. What is the name of your country?

Answers may vary

Name the country that is both one of the five largest countries by size and one of the two largest by population.

China

Write the names of the three largest countries in order of their size.

1. Russia
2. Canada
3. United States

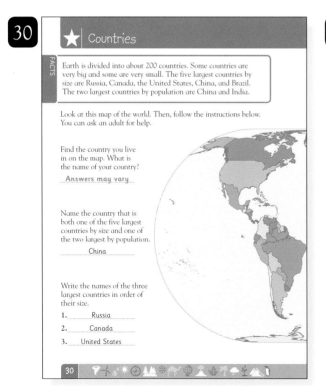

Looking at the map above, ask your child if he or she knows names of countries other than his or her own. Point to where they are on the map. You could also point to countries you have visited or have friends or relatives in.

Countries ★

FACTS

In a country, all the people share the same leaders and government. Generally, most of the people in a country speak the same language and have many things in common.

★ Borders

Sometimes, a country has a natural border that is created by an ocean or sea. Other times, a country's border can be a river or mountains. Sometimes the borders are created by people. Those man-made borders usually look like a straight line on a map.

Here is a map showing the 12 countries of South America. Draw a blue line on the border of every country. In red, color the two countries that do not have a border on an ocean or sea.

Find a map of your state or country in an atlas or on the internet. With your child, decide whether its borders are political (man-made) or natural.

Provinces and Territories ★

Some countries are divided into areas called provinces. Canada, the world's second-largest country, is divided into 10 provinces. The country also has three large areas called territories, close to the North Pole. The Yukon Territory, the Northwest Territories, and Nunavut are Canada's three territories.

Look at this map of Canada, and then follow the instructions below.

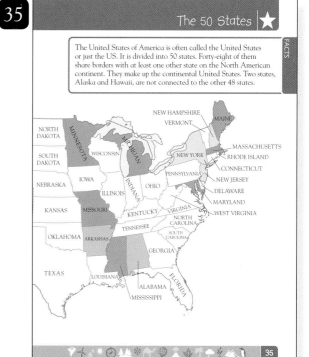

Color the only Canadian province that borders the Pacific Ocean.
Draw a warm, winter hat in the Northwest Territories.
Draw mittens in the Yukon Territory.
Draw snowflakes in Nunavut.

As an extension to this page, give your child some more facts about Canada. These may include: it has the longest coastline of any country; much of it is covered in ice; and its border with the United States is the longest border between any two countries in the world.

★ The 50 States

Some large countries, such as the United States of America, are divided into smaller areas called states. Some states, such as California and Texas, are very large. Other states, such as Rhode Island and Delaware, are very small.

Here is a map of the United States.

Color in green the four states whose names start with the word "New."

The names of eight states begin with the letter "M." Color them blue.

The names of four states begin with an "A." Color them red.

If you live in the US, put a check (✔) on your state. If you do not, check (✔) the state you would most like to visit.
Answers may vary

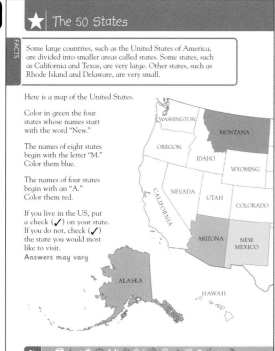

After looking at the map of the United States, close the book and encourage your child to recall the names of at least five states. Give hints if your child cannot remember any names.

The 50 States ★

The United States of America is often called the United States or just the US. It is divided into 50 states. Forty-eight of them share borders with at least one other state on the North American continent. They make up the continental United States. Two states, Alaska and Hawaii, are not connected to the other 48 states.

★ Cities

A city is a place where many people live near each other. In a city, there are many big buildings, houses, schools, parks, and roads. A city has museums, sports teams, theaters, and many things for people to do. Cities are large places, so there are many ways to travel in a city. People living in cities mostly work in offices and factories, not on farms or agricultural land.

Circle the different ways people travel in a city.
Cross out the ways people do not usually travel in a city.
Put a check (✓) next to the ways you would like to travel when you are in a city. **Answers may vary**

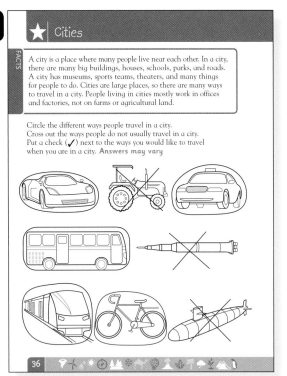

Ask your child to think of more differences between the city and the country. In addition to the differences between the buildings and transportation, ask him or her about the animals and plants you might see outside the city.

Large Cities ★

Cities come in different sizes. Some cities are very large, with millions of people. Other cities are not as large. A map can show you which cities are large and which cities are small. On a map, the names of the largest cities have the biggest letters.

Here is a map of three states in the US—California, Oregon, and Washington. Circle the names of the large cities in these states.

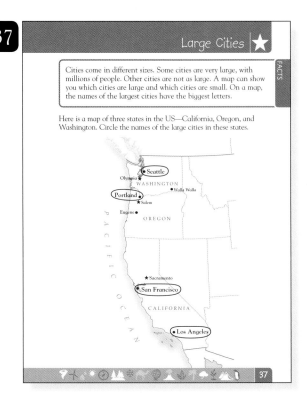

Ask your child if he or she can think of some good things about living in a big city. Then ask if he or she can think of any drawbacks to city life.

★ Capital Cities

Every country has a capital city. Leaders and the government meet in the capital city to do their work. States and provinces have capital cities, too. Capitals are not always the largest cities in a state or country. They are shown on a map by a dot that is different from the dots showing other cities.

Here is a map of the US showing three states—California, Oregon, and Washington. Circle the capital city of each state.
Hint: In this map, the capitals are marked by stars.

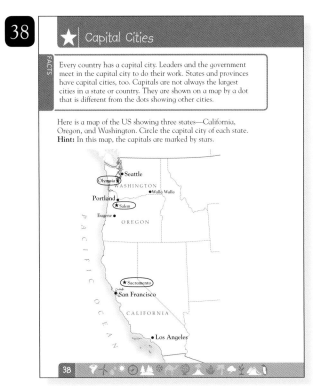

As extra information, you could tell your child that none of the five most populated cities in the United States—New York, Los Angeles, Chicago, Houston, and Philadelphia—is a state capital. Ask them if they know the capital of the United States.

Towns ★

A town is an area where people live near each other. It is smaller than a city and usually has smaller buildings. A town also has fewer people than a city. Many people choose to live in towns because they do not want to live in a big city.

Check (✓) the pictures of places you would find in a town.
Put an ✗ next to the pictures of places you would find in a city.

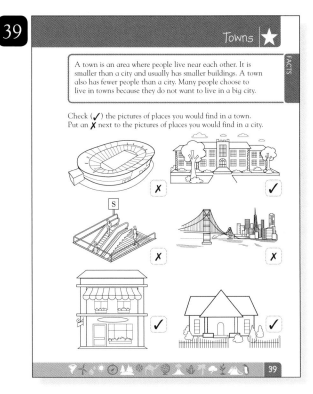

Invite your child to think of some of the good things about living in a town. Then, ask if he or she can think of any drawbacks to life in a town.

★ Map Keys and Symbols

Maps use symbols to show different kinds of buildings and other features. These symbols are usually pictures that represent the things that they show. All the symbols used on a map, and what they represent, are shown in a map key.

Match each map symbol to the word it is showing.

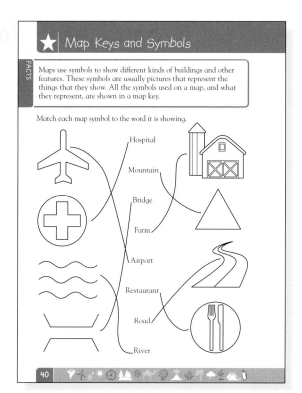

Hospital
Mountain
Bridge
Farm
Airport
Restaurant
Road
River

Next time you're outside with your child, point out road signs with symbols on them, such as a bicycle, bus, pedestrians, or an uppercase **P** or **H**. Ask your child if he or she can figure out what the signs are referring to.

A Park Map ★

A map can help you find your way around a place, such as a park. The park map on this page uses symbols to tell people what activities they can do in the park.

Using the words from the box, label each symbol on the map with what that symbol represents. Then, use the compass rose to help you answer the questions below the map.

| Snack bar | Gift shop | Parking lot | Bathroom |
| Park office | Swimming pool | Playground | |

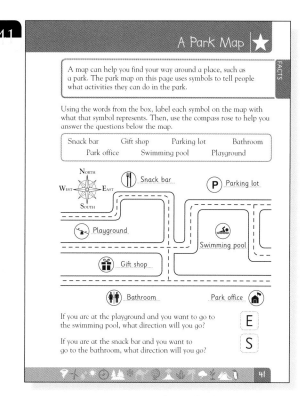

Snack bar
Parking lot
Playground
Swimming pool
Gift shop
Bathroom
Park office

If you are at the playground and you want to go to the swimming pool, what direction will you go? **E**

If you are at the snack bar and you want to go to the bathroom, what direction will you go? **S**

On your next visit to a park, study the park's map and accompanying key with your child. Ask your child to then direct you to the places you want to visit in the park.

★ A Nature Map

A nature map tells you about an area of land. Each of the symbols in the key shows a different part of the natural world. The map helps you plan where you want to go.

Using the words from the box, label the different kinds of places from the natural world that are shown on the map. Then, use the compass rose to help you answer the questions below the map.

| Beach | Waterfall | Forest | Mountains |
| Hills | Lake | River | |

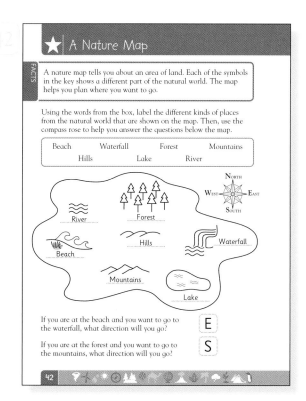

River
Forest
Hills
Waterfall
Beach
Mountains
Lake

If you are at the beach and you want to go to the waterfall, what direction will you go? **E**

If you are at the forest and you want to go to the mountains, what direction will you go? **S**

As an extra fun exercise, ask your child to draw his or her own symbol for a volcano.

A Neighborhood Map ★

A neighborhood map often uses pictures of buildings as its symbols. This kind of map is helpful for finding the places you want to visit in a town.

Imagine you are traveling from your home to your school. You are going to make a few stops on the way. You are going to stop at these places in the order given in the word box below.

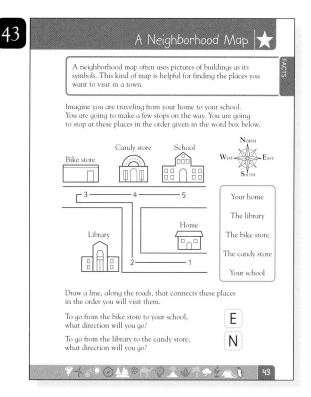

Bike store
Candy store
School
Library
Home

Your home
The library
The bike store
The candy store
Your school

Draw a line, along the roads, that connects these places in the order you will visit them.

To go from the bike store to your school, what direction will you go? **E**

To go from the library to the candy store, what direction will you go? **N**

To start a memory game, ask your child to tell you about his or her journey to school each day, describing some of the buildings along the route. If this is too difficult, offer hints.

★ A School Map

FACTS

Not all maps use picture symbols. In this map of a school, each of the different areas uses letters to tell you what you can find there.

Point at each location on the map and say its name aloud, using the key to find its name. Circle the names of your two favorite places. Then, use the compass rose to help you answer the questions below the map. **Answers may vary**

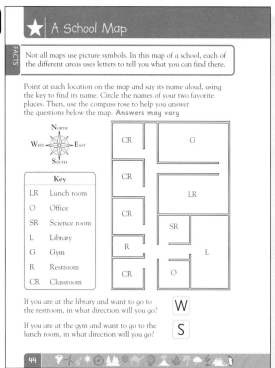

If you are at the library and want to go to the restroom, in what direction will you go? **W**

If you are at the gym and want to go to the lunch room, in what direction will you go? **S**

Invite your child to describe all the different rooms in which he or she has classes in at school. Ask him or her to describe the location, such as "upstairs" or "next to the playground" of each classroom.

Map Your Bedroom ★

FACTS

A map is a plan that can help you describe a place. Everyone can make a map. Look at the world around you. You can use simple symbols or letters to describe a place to other people. You can show the things they will find there.

Make a map of your bedroom by using any of the symbols in the key below. Draw them in the box and label them. You can add your own symbols for anything in your room that is not in the key.

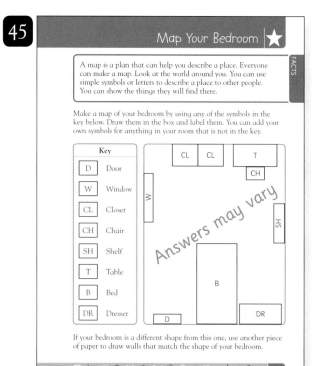

If your bedroom is a different shape from this one, use another piece of paper to draw walls that match the shape of your bedroom.

As an extra exercise, let your child draw a map of his or her ideal, or "dream," bedroom. It can be any size and include anything your child wants in it. Encourage his or her imagination.

★ Map Your Classroom

FACTS

A classroom is a place to learn. The objects in a classroom help children learn together.

Make a map of your classroom in the box below, using the symbols in the key. Create your own symbols for anything in your classroom that is missing from the key.

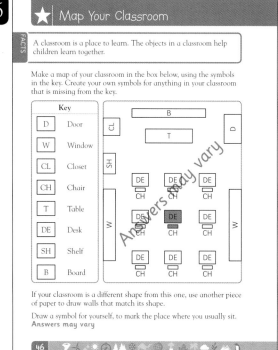

If your classroom is a different shape from this one, use another piece of paper to draw walls that match its shape.

Draw a symbol for yourself, to mark the place where you usually sit. **Answers may vary**

Are all the classrooms in your child's school the same? Ask your child to think of some differences between the various classrooms in which he or she has classes.

Map Your Neighborhood ★

FACTS

There are all kinds of neighborhoods. Some neighborhoods have many different kinds of buildings. Others may have very few buildings. A map of your neighborhood can help you understand the things you find there. It can help you describe your neighborhood to a friend.

Imagine the square in the middle of the box below is the home you live in. Draw your neighborhood around where you live. Include squares for buildings like a school or a supermarket.

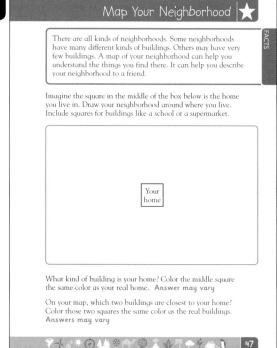

What kind of building is your home? Color the middle square the same color as your real home. **Answer may vary**

On your map, which two buildings are closest to your home? Color those two squares the same color as the real buildings. **Answers may vary**

Discuss differences between your neighborhood and that of a friend or relative. Are all neighborhoods the same?